Inspiring
Women
Every Day

January
PRESENCE
....
CHRIS LEONARD

February
RESTORING OUR
CUTTING EDGE
....
ANNE LE TISSIER

Plus... 'Be Inspired' article, CWR Today
pages and CWR Ministry Events

MIX
Paper from
responsible sources
FSC® C015900
www.fsc.org

WAVERLEY ABBEY
RESOURCES
Trading name of **CWR**

Chris Leonard

Chris Leonard leads many creative writing workshops and holidays and, with a degree in English and Theology, she has had 21 books published. Chris and her husband live in Surrey, England, and have two grown-up children and three young grandchildren. She can be contacted on chrisleonardwriting.uk

Anne Le Tissier

Anne has a passion to disciple Christians in the ongoing walk with God. She is the author of a number of Christian books and has written a variety of Bible study notes and magazine articles. She also speaks around the country, as well as being on the Inspiring Women team. To relax she loves to read, grow her own vegetables, hike in the hills and cook special meals for family and friends. Anne also dreams of one day becoming a beekeeper!

Waverley Abbey Resources is the trading name of CWR.
Copyright © CWR 2020. Published by CWR, Waverley Abbey House, Waverley Lane, Farnham, Surrey GU9 8EP, UK. Tel: 01252 784700 Email: mail@cwr.org.uk
Registered Charity No. 294387. Registered Limited Company No. 1990308.
Front cover image: Adobestock.com
Concept development, editing, design and production by CWR. Printed in England by Linney. All rights reserved. No part of this publication may be reproduced, stored in a retrieval system, or transmitted, in any form or by any means, electronic, mechanical, photocopying, recording or otherwise, without the prior permission in writing of CWR.
Unless otherwise indicated, all Scripture references are from the Holy Bible, New International Version® Anglicised, NIV® Copyright © 1979, 1984, 2011 by Biblica, Inc.® Used by permission. All rights reserved worldwide. Scripture quotations marked The Message are taken from THE MESSAGE, copyright © 1993, 2002, 2018 by Eugene H. Peterson. Used by permission of NavPress. All rights reserved. Represented by Tyndale House Publishers, Inc. NLT: The Holy Bible, New Living Translation, copyright © 1996, 2004, 2015 by Tyndale House Foundation. Used by permission of Tyndale House Publishers, Inc., Carol Stream, Illinois 60188. All rights reserved.

Presence

CHRIS LEONARD

Have you noticed how, at the start of a new year, the media often ceases to reflect on past horrors, instead putting their hope in the change of calendar and potential resolutions? The effectiveness of new year's resolutions does little to either assuage my fears for the future or satisfy my longing for a fresh start. On the other hand, all my worries tend to fall into perspective when I know that God is God – and He is with us.

One January, my husband and I drove through snow to reach my mother-in-law, who lay unconscious and, we thought, dying in hospital. Only God knows whether she heard me reading her favourite psalm but, at that sad and stressful time, its words reminded our family of God's presence in that busy hospital ward. He was in charge and He was Mum's Saviour. He was also, tangibly, 'our refuge and strength, an ever-present help in trouble' (v1).

Over the next month we'll be exploring the theme of 'presence' together. What is the presence of God and what difference does it make, to ourselves and to others? How do we know He's present with us, amidst turmoil and distress? Is He there, even when we don't feel His presence? If He seems to have departed, what do we do? How can we be more fully present to Him? Whoever wrote the ancient song we call Psalm 46 provided deep insights that still resonate now. This New Year's Day, take time to drink deep from God's refreshing pool. Not mere champagne, but the water of eternal life that wells up from the deep source of everything. Read the psalm again and let God speak directly to you, in whatever circumstances you find yourself.

Psalm 46

'He says, "Be still and know that I am God…" The LORD Almighty is with us' (vv10–11)

For prayer and reflection

Still yourself before God. Breathe out your worries; breathe in His grace. Say, 'I am here to meet with You, Lord. Help me simply to rest here in Your presence now.'

Holy ground

....

Exodus 3:1–15

'God said, "I will be with you… I AM WHO I AM… say to the Israelites: "I AM has sent me to you."' (vv12,14)

I t seems so unlikely – God turns an obscure patch of wilderness into holy ground by revealing His presence in a flaming bush. Then insists a fugitive murderer-turned-shepherd undertake a 'mission impossible' on His behalf. God's fiercely burning presence frightens and disturbs, rather than comforts Moses. Ultimately, God will bring salvation – but Moses seems even more afraid to look at Him than to confront Pharaoh.

God's name, His identity, is 'I AM'. He is, was and always will be present tense. 'I AM' was present with Moses' ancestors (v15) and will be present when Moses seeks his race's deliverance from Egypt. Think of times when God has been present with you throughout this century so far. God, unlike us, is eternally present.

We don't always recognise that presence, let alone judder to a halt before a terrifying apparition as Moses did. But if God is always present, surely we too are standing (or sitting) on holy ground right now. This weekend, you might want to reflect on the famous song lyrics, 'Be still, for the presence of the Lord, the holy one, is here', to help you draw closer to Him.

....

Optional further reading

Psalm 100

His presence **everywhere**

Psalm 139

'Where can I flee from your presence? If I go up to the heavens… [or] in the depths, you are there.'
(vv7–8)

This week we're asking: what is the presence of the Lord like? He may not be physically visible, audible or touchable, but Scripture shows Him making His presence known in various ways to different people in diverse situations. There are constants too. Whatever we may sense or feel, God is omnipresent – His presence is everywhere. Another theological adjective for God is 'prevenient', meaning wherever we may go, however deep, dark and hostile our environment appears to us, God has been there beforehand – and is still there. A third word is 'omniscient' – He sees everything, including us, even our darkest secrets.

In Psalm 139, David expresses and then applies all this. Read it again, looking out for instances of those three constants and thinking about times in your own life when you've experienced similar things. You may not have been conscious of His presence in your mother's womb, but God was, is and will always be with you, leading you 'in the way everlasting'.

Usually, God's presence is not 'manifest' (revealed, or on show) in the most obvious or tangible of ways. Nevertheless I've sensed and experienced it in churches, by the sea, in the woods, up mountains and on the London Underground; in an exam hall, a prison and the anteroom to an operating theatre; in the heat of Ghana and even on a ship, despite being seasick, homesick and cold. I don't always *feel* He's with me but, like the psalmist, I know there's no place, time or circumstance where He isn't present.

If you've never read Francis Thompson's long poem, 'The Hound of Heaven', do take a look at it online.

For prayer and reflection

Lord, You are amazing. We can't begin to understand how wide and long and high and deep You are, inhabiting everywhere, eternally. We worship You. Amen.

Presence **with us**

Exodus 33:7–14

'The LORD replied,
"My Presence will
go with you"' (v14)

'Jesus' means 'Saviour', and 'Immanuel' means 'God with us' (see Matt. 1:21–23). For three decades, Jesus was present, as a man, to a few thousand people. After His ascension, the Father sent the Holy Spirit, who remains with us, as close and invisible as our breath, or the wind in our hair. I've never experienced God's presence as moving pillars of cloud or fire as Moses did, nor glimpsed the retreating glory of His back (v23). But then Moses had no Jewish scriptures, nor accounts of Jesus to show him what God is like. He had to find out directly for himself and then tell others, whereas we can see the evidence of God's presence – for example, in the changed lives of Christians, through someone's supernatural wisdom and through anointed preachers, story sharers or worship leaders.

How can we be sure that God is with us as individuals? By faith in His promises, of course, but occasionally we need something tangible – a manifest sign of His presence. We might not see anything as dramatic as Moses did: God has gentler ways of making His presence felt. For example, a friend told me how, one day, she'd had enough. She'd shouted, first at the dog and then at God. He'd been asking her to do some things that a debilitating illness had made her feel utterly incapable of doing. After a while, though alone, she felt an arm around her shoulders and a voice saying: 'It's all right. I know!' – just as a parent might to a young child having a meltdown. She knew she was loved, and He was in charge. If you've known such tangible signs, do write them down, remember and share them.

**For prayer
and reflection**

Lord, may we not
only know Your
transforming
presence with us,
but be so
distinguished by it
that we make Your
glory visible to
others. Amen.

WAVERLEY ABBEY

Transforming lives

Waverley Abbey's vision is to enable people to experience personal transformation through applying God's Word to their lives and relationships.

Our Bible-based training and resources help people around the world to:

- Grow in their walk with God
- Understand and apply Scripture to their lives
- Resource themselves and their church
- Develop pastoral care and counselling skills
- Train for leadership
- Strengthen relationships, marriage and family life and much more.

Our insightful writers provide daily Bible reading notes and engaging resources for everyone, and our experienced course designers and presenters have gained an international reputation for excellence and effectiveness.

Our Waverley Abbey House training and conference centre in Surrey, England, provides excellent facilities in idyllic settings – ideal for both learning and spiritual refreshment.

waverleyabbey.org

Terrifying, powerful

'Who can stand in the presence of the Lord, this holy God? To whom will the ark go up from here?' (v20)

'E piphany' means 'revelation'. The Christian feast of Epiphany today celebrates Jesus' presence being revealed, not only to His chosen people, but to foreign magi. God's presence among us – how wonderful! Yet, as manifest in the Old Testament, it can also terrify with lightning bolts – dangerous, unpredictable, inexplicable. Today's story disturbs me. Philistine enemies had seized Israel's sacred ark of the covenant where, it was believed, God had taken up residence. Now that the Philistines were sending it back in fear, the Israelites, out harvesting Beth Shemesh's fields, rejoiced and worshipped God by sacrificing their working oxen and used the wood from their harvest-carts to burn the offerings. But then God slaughtered 70 of them for 'looking into' His ark! Why? For daring to pull it apart, trying to pry into God's secrets and seize His 'magic' power for themselves. 'Quick!' they said. 'The ark's too dangerous for us – let someone else have it. They're welcome to the lethal presence of God!'

Through Jesus' sacrifice, by contrast, God invites us to draw ever closer to Him without fear – but do we sometimes become a little over-familiar, taking His astounding presence for granted, as we might that of a dear human friend? It's appropriate to feel awe in the presence of the most holy God, the Lord and creator of everything. That's what I've learnt from this story. His holy presence manifests not only His moral perfection but also His power. He's set apart, utterly superior to us. Having grasped that, I can only wonder the more at His love constantly reaching out to us!

In the Lord's **presence**

Hannah, Samuel's mother, sent her only son to serve God in the Temple. Unlike the priest's sons, Samuel didn't hold the Lord in contempt nor take Him for granted (as I, growing up in a Christian home, have done at times). Samuel served faithfully and 'continued to grow in stature and in favour with the LORD and with people' (v26). In the following chapter, he's still just a boy when God manifests Himself, changes his life, and, through him, that of Eli's sons and thousands of His people.

One Christmas, when I was about twelve, I was unwell so, while my parents and brother cleared up in the kitchen after lunch, I sat alone in the lounge. There, in the quietness, God's presence filled the room – and me – with peace, joy, awe and love. I come from a loving Christian family. God was always there, but this was such a special moment – His presence and love for me more evident, more 'real' to me, than ever before. Something similar happened after some sight-seeing on a family day out in St Albans, Hertfordshire, UK. Following our picnic lunch, I sat quietly for a moment in the cathedral. There God's presence became so strong. I wanted to hold on to it forever. A piece of straw from the chair where I was sitting had worked loose, so I pocketed it to keep as a reminder – then lost it, of course. But there's no need for reminders of that eternal moment, simply sitting in God's evident presence. It's become a foundational part of me. Rarely have I experienced it with such intensity, but I believe that He builds on times when we do; they help us to grow in Him. Experiencing His strong love is the wellspring to our loving others better.

1 Samuel 2:12–26

'the boy Samuel grew up in the presence of the LORD.' (v21)

For prayer and reflection

Recall any 'eternal moments' when you've become especially aware of God's presence, whether as a child or as an adult. Give thanks and ask God to keep growing you.

Saving presence

2 Corinthians 4:1–18

'[Father God] will also raise us with Jesus and present us with you to himself.' (v14)

Though bringing righteous anger and judgment on some occasions, often God's presence in the Old Testament is associated with His protection, shelter, rescue, joy, comfort, love and guidance. We'll look more at those things later this month. But, before that, I want to jump to the New Testament and to Paul's writing about something literally earth-shattering that will happen in the future – perhaps the fullest expression of what God's presence is like.

'To present' means 'to place before'. On the final Day of Judgment, God will raise everyone from the dead as surely as He raised Jesus, and will present (place us before) Himself. He knows everything we've ever done or thought. Have you ever been presented in a legal or royal court? I'd be shaking! How would we feel in the presence of His Majesty, King of kings, Lord of lords, the Creator and Judge of all – you and me there, together with scriptural giants like Paul and Moses, Peter and David? Oh, and Jesus. He'll be there too. He who, when present and visible in the flesh, said: 'I did not come to judge the world, but to save the world' (John 12:47). Because Jesus died and was raised for us, those of us who know Him will be saved – not despite Father God, but because His Father sent Him. In the same way the Father has sent us the Holy Spirit to keep us walking closely with Him.

All three persons of the Trinity work to save us – from sin, from Satan and from ourselves. Or, rather, to restore the selves we were created to be – living in constantly present, loving relationship with God and with each other.

For prayer and reflection

Worship God now using these words from Revelation 7:10: 'Salvation belongs to our God, who sits on the throne, and to the Lamb'.

Jesus' presence

·····················

Mark 1:14–32

'A new teaching – and with authority! He even gives orders to impure spirits and they obey him.' (v27)

What do we mean when we say that a person – an actor or the head of an organisation perhaps – has 'presence'? That they command our full attention and act with authority? Search today's passage for signs of what Jesus' earthly presence was like and how it affected different people. What made many 'ordinary' folk (though not those from the town where He grew up) believe Him, flock to Him and even give up everything to follow Him?

What made demons flee? What made Herod and the religious rulers – who thought they were the ones possessing presence and authority – attack Jesus? What made the blind see Him as someone special and the hopeless know that He could forgive and heal? Imagine you were there, meeting Him along with all these people. What would His presence have felt like and how might it have affected you? Talk with Him about it.

Perhaps search online and take a look at the anonymous sixteenth-century poem 'Preparations' – it starts: 'Yet if His Majesty, our sovereign Lord...' Imagine Jesus coming in person to your home today. What difference would His presence make there?

·····················

Optional further reading
Matthew 7:28–8:29; Mark 2:1–12; 10:46–52

His presence **gone**?

Genesis 4:1–16

'So Cain went out from the LORD's presence and lived in the land of Nod, east of Eden.' (v16)

The chapter preceding today's reading tells how Adam and Eve's rebellion led to banishment from Eden. No longer did they enjoy a close relationship with God, who had walked with them 'in the garden in the cool of the day' (Gen. 3:8). But was His presence, in any sense, still with them? Maybe, or why would their murderous son Cain absent himself from it (or think he does), becoming 'a restless wanderer on the earth' (v12)?

We've already ascertained that we cannot flee from God's presence: '"Who can hide in secret places so that I cannot see them?" declares the LORD. "Do not I fill heaven and earth?"' (Jer. 23:24). Have you tried fleeing? I have, one miserable time. Jonah did too. It doesn't work. We can disobey Him and deny the relationship, but He sticks around. And, as Simon Peter said, only He has the words of eternal life (John 6:68). Of course, He has given us free will, which means we always have the choice to turn our backs on Him.

What, though, if we haven't fled or transgressed? If we long for Him, yet can't sense His presence with us, for an hour, a year or even a decade? A bereaved mother and daughter once told me their grief made them too numb to feel anything, let alone God's presence. Does the Bible offer any comfort or reassurance when God appears absent? Yes, it does – so often that it's clear the experience is not uncommon. 'Epiphany' means God showing Himself, appearing, becoming manifest or conspicuous; but He hides Himself too – as from Job (13:24). Several psalmists and many post-biblical saints also have written of this 'dark night of the soul'.

For prayer and reflection

Lord, thank You for the light of Your presence. Have mercy on all who stumble in the darkness of Your seeming absence today. Amen.

Waverley Abbey College

'We are all on a journey of discovery when it comes to the matters of the soul, and it is always good to question what we are saying and doing in relation to helping people and their problems.' – Selwyn Hughes, Founder of CWR

Our programmes equip students with the skills and knowledge to release their God-given potential to operate in roles that help people.

Central to all of our teaching is the Waverley Integrative Framework. Built on 50 years of experience, the model emphasises the importance of genuineness, unconditional acceptance and empathy in relationships.

Counselling

As society begins to realise the extent of its brokenness, we continue to recognise the need to train people to support those who are struggling with everyday life, providing training to equip individuals to become professional counsellors.

Whatever their starting point in academic learning, we have a pathway to help all students on their academic journey.

Spiritual Formation

For those wanting to be better equipped to help others on their spiritual journey, this programme provides robust and effective Spiritual Formation training. Students engage with theology, psychology, social sciences, historical studies, counselling, leadership studies and psychotherapy.

For more information about all of our course offerings available, visit **waverleyabbeycollege.ac.uk** or come along to a free Open Day.

Leaving His presence

Mark 10:17–27

"'Then come, follow me.' The man's face fell. He went away sad, because he had great wealth.' (vv21–22)

Did Jesus' face fall too as His extraordinary invitation to follow in His presence was rejected in favour of mere wealth? Mark tells us He loved the man, as He loves us all. Many rejected Him, though. People from Nazareth, where He grew up, refused to believe Him to be anything special. Most Jewish religious leaders rubbished His claims and authority. His teaching about 'eating' His flesh and 'drinking' His blood caused 'many of his disciples' to cease following Him (John 6:66). Judas, one of the Twelve, baulked at His unusual strategy to defeat the powers that be – and betrayed Him. What wonderful opportunities all these had to be with Him! Yet they walked away. I wonder, would I have been any different?

Do you sometimes think you know best – choosing to ignore hard teaching or difficult truths about yourself, or preferring your own comfort and security to following, serving and obeying God? Have you ever forsaken His people, their ways of life, their truths, to follow those of a different crowd? Is anything more important to you than Jesus? If, like me, you answer 'yes' to any of these, maybe it's time for a bit of a spiritual audit: but not one we do ourselves – we need an auditor. Let's invite the Holy Spirit to show us what we are walking towards instead of Jesus. Remember, even if we've 'broken God's law', He won't condemn. Remember too that Jesus loved the rich young ruler. I wonder if He sought him out, or sent others to do so later? Because that's what Father, Son and Holy Spirit do – they keep providing opportunities for us to draw closer. They seek and save the lost.

For prayer and reflection

Through our eyes, the world and our lives seem dark; through eyes of faith, everything's different, brighter. Do you need a change of perspective today?

His presence **vital**

**Exodus
33:1–6,15–17**

magine being Moses, leading people who rebel. God responds to their rebellion by saying that, though He'll keep His promise of land – and even of His angels to drive out their enemies – He won't go with them! Horrified, Moses knows that without God they are nothing. After the people repent, he pleads with 'I AM': 'How will anyone know that you are pleased with me and with your people unless you go with us? What else will distinguish me and your people from all the other people on the face of the earth?' (v16). God relents. Moses converses with Him, as a friend, and the people watch as he does so. Then he sees God's glory, goodness and His back, if not His face. God is with Moses all right, evidenced in that the visible signs of God's presence and leadership – His pillars of fire and cloud – continue to guide Israel on their long journey.

Penny had an established ministry in England when God called her husband to mission tasks in another continent. Amidst strangers with a different culture, customs, officialdom and language, the excitement of God's promises shrivelled. What was He doing? At least her husband had his work; she... nothing except faith in a God whose presence didn't always feel evident. But, in time, her relationship with Him deepened, as did the couple's relationships with their children. God's presence and those relationships – all Penny had left – became the most precious and important things in her life. And then God restored her own preaching ministry with hugely added power, first in a language with which she struggled and later with joyous freedom back home in England.

"'Moses said to him, 'If your Presence does not go with us, do not send us up from here.'" (v15)

For prayer and reflection

'Unless the LORD builds the house, the builders labour in vain' (Psalm 127:1). Keep us in Your presence, Lord. Amen.

Crisis! **Where** is He?

1 John 3:18–24

'This is how we know that we belong to the truth and how we set our hearts at rest in his presence' (v19)

W hen crises strike, at times I have felt God's supernatural peace. More typically, rising panic consumes me. Desperate to find solutions, I end up feeling fearful and helpless. Where was God when I needed Him? How could I set my heart at rest in His presence when He appeared to have abandoned me? And what chance for me anyway if Jesus' disciples, caught in a fearsome storm, panicked, despite being able to see Him right there in the boat with them (Luke 8:22–25)? After failing to control their vessel, terror drove them to call on Him. Then Jesus sorted everything in an instant, though not before asking – where was their faith? Where was mine? Is it I who am not present to Him?

Then it occurred to me... faith! Times of crisis test whether I believe in my head only or show it through my actions. God knows that our learning to do the latter can be a slow process. Crises give us opportunities to learn to trust Him more – to understand that we belong to Him, to put our confidence in Him and to do, not as our fear dictates, but as the Holy Spirit leads us.

And yet... do I call on Him first? Not often. Instead I'll seek other solutions, perhaps online. I might go to friends or draw on my own puny resources. After exhausting all these, I'll descend to becoming self-centred, self-pitying and self-protective, when what He asks is that I'll keep doing the loving thing. With perfect timing, that's what a friend did for me recently, phoning me to say she's praying, even offering help, though she's in the middle of far more of a crisis than I am.

For prayer and reflection

Lord, of course You're here always, as You promised. Thank You that, as John says, we live in You and You in us. We'd be lost without You! Amen.

Presence lost – and **found**

Luke 15:4–31

'Rejoice with me; I have found my lost sheep.' (v6)

There is a common distress for the woman, shepherd and father in these three familiar stories. They agonise and search, no doubt distraught but also clinging to hope. Imagine the joy when the lost are found! There's partying in Jesus' stories, but there's also the simmering resentment from the stay-at-home son. And imagine the attitude of the 99 sheep left in the fold as their shepherd disappears from sight: 'Silly Tilly, she should know better than to keep wandering off. All very well to keep trotting into danger but doesn't she realise what it means for the rest of the flock, stuck here in this sheepfold? When Shepherd goes off to look for her, who's to guard us from wolves or sheep-stealers? Who'll lead us to grazing or to water? It's so hot, crowded and smelly in here! Noisy too, what with everyone baa-ing their grumbles. I used to think Him a good shepherd. Now I'm not sure!'

I hold the sense of God's presence in church services precious. But what if they are disturbed by any one of the interruptions that come with being part of a community? What if an anointed preacher, worship leader or wise counsellor is called away elsewhere?

They say the Church exists primarily for the benefit of its non-members. Jesus didn't tell us to remain safe in 'sheepfolds', however 'holy': He commissioned us to go and make disciples across the world. Maybe that's where His presence is most tangible – with the lost who are being sought and found. I've known the reality of His presence strongest inside a prison, when those incarcerated hear of His forgiveness and ask for His help in transforming their lives.

For prayer and reflection

I know You're everywhere, Lord, and You're in me! Help me recognise Your presence – and activity – in every interaction I have with people and situations today. Amen.

Weekend

Presence affecting us

....

Psalm 16

'You make known to me the path of life; you will fill me with joy in your presence' (v11)

D
o you act differently depending on which people are present? I think most of us do, at least to some extent. For example, think about the boss appearing suddenly at work; or when someone you hardly know turns up at your home. We might behave formally, even timidly, before barristers and judges in a courtroom, but 'let our hair down' with good friends at a party.

So, given that God's with us when we're at our worst as well as at our best, how does His constant presence affect us? Many scriptures tell us to fear Him, but the Bible also says that His perfect love casts out fear, that He is a loving Father to us, a comforter, a Saviour...

Try to take a moment to think and pray it through this weekend. Remember, 'There is no fear in love. But perfect love drives out fear, because fear has to do with punishment. The one who fears is not made perfect in love' (1 John 4:18). Do you feel guilt or affirmation in His presence? Joy, excitement, expectation? Does His compassion for others affect you, spurring you to action?

....

Optional further reading

Psalm 63 – and other psalms, noting how God's presence affected the writers.

God's Plan for your Wellbeing

NEW book and Church Programme

Journey with Dave Smith through this 50-day
devotional and the the story of the prophet
Elijah, as you explore God's plan for your
wellbeing. Dave also shares some of the lesson's
he has learnt in order to help you, your Church,
or your small group achieve the physical,
emotional and spiritual balance that enables
you to flourish for God and for good.

Find out more at
waverleyabbeyresources.org/GPFYW

Responding to presence

Genesis 45:1–18

'they were terrified at his presence.' (v3)

What drama! Imagine that you and all your family are starving, so you make the long journey to seek help from the nearest super-power nation. Will they be friendly? You'll be lucky even to get a hearing! But you're ushered in, your heart in your mouth, to put your case to the second highest in the land. He sends everyone else away and sobs loudly before revealing that, years ago, he was the brother whom you and your siblings sold into slavery.

The brothers have so many reasons to be terrified in Joseph's presence, but something has transformed him. No longer the arrogant upstart, dreaming of all his brothers bowing at his feet – now he's kissing them, welcoming them with tears of joy and begging the entire family to come and live near him. He's suffered greatly – his brothers don't know the half of it. Yet he tells them it was God, not they, who sent him to Egypt, in order to save their lives and those of future generations. Ultimately, it's not Joseph's status and position of power that counts here but his character. What counts is who he is, or rather what time spent in God's presence – whether in the prison or the palace – has enabled him to become.

How do you behave in the presence of great secular power and influence? How does that differ from your attitude in the presence of someone humble, perhaps, but holy – someone who lives extraordinarily close to God? Which would you rather be with? Which would you rather be? Spend some time with God, considering all the implications for your life, your ambitions, the company you keep and who you follow.

For prayer and reflection

Lord, may our awe in Your presence decrease our fear of human power. Thank You for being full of grace and love. Amen.

People's presence – and absence

Philippians 2:12–30

'not only in my presence, but now much more in my absence… work out your salvation… God… works in you.' (vv12–13)

How Paul must have longed to visit and nurture the young churches that he had planted. With no prospect of release from prison in Rome, he must have rejoiced when good news of them arrived, along with the rare opportunity to communicate by letter. His pain becomes our gain as his words, dating from those early decades of Christianity, still speak to us all these years later.

Paul's presence had provoked change in the lives of the Philippians to whom he wrote, and now he had evidence that the God who was with him in Rome was equally in Philippi, teaching the believers His ways, continuing to mature them as His fruitful disciples. Something similar happened after the Cultural Revolution expelled all foreign missionaries who had planted new churches in China. The country's borders remained closed to outsiders, though rumours filtered through of terrible persecutions. The missionaries must have feared that all their work had been in vain. Yet when China reopened its borders, they found that numbers following Christ had increased by many millions. God's presence can't be shut out. Soon, it is believed, there will be more Christians in China than in any other nation.

Do you worry about someone you long to be with or help? Does access seem impossible? Read the passage again, looking for Paul's heart and attitudes around issues of presence… and absence. Perhaps you believe your relationship with God would improve if only a certain minister were leading and preaching at your church again? Good teachers and leaders help – but it's God we really need!

For prayer and reflection

Lord, we feel helpless when someone we love is suffering at a distance. We can do nothing except thank You for being with them, as we hold them up before You now. Amen.

Presence **manifest**

**Philippians
4:1–9**

'And the peace
of God, which
transcends all
understanding,
will guard your
hearts and your
minds in Christ
Jesus.' (v7)

S omeone once said to me, 'God doesn't send us peace, He *is* our peace!' His presence, including His peace, joy, hope etc, is both around us and within. Sometimes He reminds us of this in surprising ways.

My artist friend Marina lives and works near London. Lately, concerns for her ailing parents back in Croatia have grown. When a phone call announced that her mother was in hospital after a serious fall, she panicked. 'God, what do I do?' Drawn to the National Gallery, and then towards to a medieval picture she'd never seen before, she read the words painted there, translated as 'My peace I give to you; My peace I leave with you.' She felt that peace! Helping her parents could be disruptive and physically and emotionally exhausting, but God showed her the very best solution for them. Deuteronomy 33:27 says, 'The eternal God is your refuge, and underneath are the everlasting arms' and Marina affirms the truth of that. 'Though worries came, God's extraordinary peace and presence undergirded and supported me through it all,' she says.

Paul, writing to the Philippians from prison, says this in verse 9: 'Whatever you have learned or received or heard from me, or seen in me – put it into practice. And the God of peace will be with you.' Think of all you've learnt of God from other Christians you've met or listened to over the years. Whether or not they are still with you, are you still following the ways of God you saw in and through their example? In what surprising ways has God made His presence manifest to you, making a real difference, as seeing that picture did for Marina?

**For prayer
and reflection**

**Lord, thank You!
All that is true,
noble, right, pure,
lovely, excellent
and praiseworthy
is fully present in
You – and reflected
in those who love
and follow You.
Amen.**

Affected by those present

John 8:31–47

'I am telling you what I have seen in the Father's presence' (v38)

Yesterday, we reflected on following the ways of our heavenly Father. By contrast, the religious leaders of the Jews are doing what they have heard from their father. That's father with a small 'f'. Parents aren't perfect; they get some things right and other things wrong (at least that's what my experience of being a parent tells me). And each family has its own ways – some of them help, others harm. Think back to your own upbringing, and the formative years you spent with your parents. What were the helpful attitudes, ways of thinking, speaking and doing things you absorbed from them? And what were the prejudices, fears, discouragements and so forth that may continue to have a negative effect on you?

Abraham, the father of the Jewish nation, though far from perfect, did step out most courageously in faith to follow God. Consider the spiritual influence on your life of church leaders, of Christian friends, teachers and writers. The traditions of individuals, families, nations and different religious groupings often contain a mixture of positive and negative, helpful and unhelpful, when viewed in the light of Jesus.

No church, or person, has everything right! Jesus says that it's His truth that will set us free. After all He, who has lived and still lives in His Father's presence, He alone is perfect. Learn in His presence – He may change some deep-seated beliefs and attitudes! Proverbs 3:5–6 says, 'Trust in the LORD with all your heart and lean not on your own understanding; in all your ways submit to him, and he will make your paths straight.'

For prayer and reflection

Thank You, Lord for all the good influences and godly people we've known. Free us from any unhelpful traditions we've absorbed. Help us to follow in Your ways. Amen.

Together in His presence

1 Chronicles 29:10–20

'So they all praised the LORD… they bowed down, prostrating themselves before the LORD' (v20)

I n the Old Testament, Israel often gathered in God's presence for one of two reasons: to take solemn vows or to worship. In this passage we see them doing both. What about us? Relics of such vows appear in courts of law where witnesses are asked to swear on the Bible, or in church weddings where people gather 'in the sight of God' to witness solemn vows and be warned not to separate those God joined together.

We can worship God anywhere – alone in a forest or prison cell, or on a crowded street where not another soul acknowledges Him – but it's especially powerful and faith-affirming to worship Him together with others who love Him. It's often the setting in which people re-dedicate themselves to Him too.

Walking to church alone one Sunday, my mood reflected the morning's cloudy greyness. I felt far from God's presence or help, having been preoccupied for weeks, worrying about a stressful situation. Then a sunflower in the allotments ahead drew my eyes like a small sun – round, bright and so yellow! Others nearby were all facing the same way. Sunflowers always turn to face the sun. I wondered, *How do they know its whereabouts today?* Then a layer of cloud shifted, proving the flowers' orientation correct, and God broke through my clouds too. 'I'm here. Face in the direction you know. Keep going, one step at a time.' I smiled. God knew I was walking towards church, where worshipping with others and hearing His truth would help keep me facing in the right direction. He'd sent a brief shaft of sun to spotlight those flowers. He was with me. I could trust Him.

For prayer and reflection

Keep me facing and drawing strength from You, Lord. Thank You that I'm not alone and, when I struggle, can find affirmation through others who love You too. Amen.

WAVERLEY ABBEY

Find out more online

For more information and to make purchases of new books and courses or to take a look at the college courses and training that we offer, please take a look at our websites.

 waverleyabbey.org

 waverleyabbeyresources.org

 waverleyabbeycollege.ac.uk

 waverleyabbeyhouse.org

Weekend

Fully present?

....

Psalm 27

'Wait for the LORD; be strong and take heart and wait for the LORD.' (v14)

I've found this psalm helpful when I've felt estranged from God's presence – whether beset by worries and dangers, numb with grief or simply rushed for time to spend with Him. King David asks only one thing: to 'dwell in the house of the LORD all the days of my life, to gaze on the beauty of the LORD and to seek him in his temple' (v4). But David has numerous duties, both to his family and as king. Sometimes he has to fight wars, flee or hide. He could never spend all of his time in the special tent of God's presence. Being 'fully present' in that way isn't always possible.

The situation may not change, yet David remains confident in the Lord, who has always been his helper. He declares certain truths, applying them to his past, present and future. Speaking out, to himself and anyone who will listen, he 'takes heart', finding courage, faith, hope and calm patience to wait for the Lord.

God is with you too and will prove it, in His way and His time. Meanwhile, declare the eternal truths you know, and thank Him for being your light and salvation.

....

Optional further reading

Deuteronomy 33:24–29; 1 Samuel 2:18–21,26
For a helpful expansion of mindfulness in a Christian direction, read Brian Draper's *Soulfulness* (London: Hodder & Stoughton, 2016).

Living in the light of His presence

Psalm 89:1–18

'Blessed are those who have learned to acclaim you, who walk in the light of your presence, LORD.'
(v15)

When I acclaim God in church on Sunday (whether online or in person), I believe what I'm saying or singing. Come Monday morning, though, is it still affecting the way I live my life? Am I walking in the light of His presence? How do we get what we believe from our heads into our hearts, our thoughts, our speech and our actions? Do you, like me, find that's where you struggle sometimes? I mean, I believe God is all powerful, that He is with me, is faithful, just, compassionate and loving. I believe He wants righteousness to reign in my life and everywhere. I believe that He can give me the strength, wisdom, compassion – everything necessary – to face difficult situations and people in His way. And yet, when the next challenge comes along, more often than not I withdraw into fear and self-pity, or perhaps become unreasonably cross and resentful.

A few years ago, I heard a simple prayer that I've found to be of practical help. I wish I could discipline myself to use it at regular intervals, all through every day, but I tend to remember only when facing what feels like an enormous challenge. The prayer begins with: 'Lord, You are here. Your presence fills this place. In Your presence is…' After adding whatever you feel you lack and need, such as strength, love, forgiveness, peace, or wisdom; you continue, 'In all I have to do, I give myself to You.'

'Blessed are those who have learned to acclaim you,' says the psalmist. We are blessed, not simply for ourselves but to *be* blessings. As we let God enable us to live, speak and act according to His ways, we'll shine His light into the darkness.

For prayer and reflection

Your kingdom come, Your will be done – through us Lord, by Your strength and enabling. Amen.

....

**Deuteronomy
10:1–21**

....

'set apart… to
carry the ark… to
stand before the
LORD to minister
and to pronounce
blessings in his
name.' (v8)

Carrying **presence**, speaking **blessing**

The priestly tribe of Levi were set apart to carry God's tangible presence around in that holy (and sometimes dangerous) ark; to stand before Him, ministering in worship and to 'pronounce blessings in his name'. A sermon I heard recently on this small, obscure verse answered some prayers about how I might better make Jesus' presence known.

Every follower of Jesus has a priestly function. 'You are… a royal priesthood… that you may declare the praises of him who called you out of darkness into his wonderful light' (1 Pet. 2:9). That means we have been given authority to stand in His presence and to pronounce blessings in His name. This revelation is transforming my prayer-life and the way I minister to others. I've found giving a prayerful, specific blessing to people who don't yet know Jesus to be acceptable, as well as powerful. God wants to bless, always – to grow all the good that He created in someone, to heal their wounds and relationships, to give wisdom, guide towards righteousness, wholeness and integrity, and to welcome them into His presence.

Instead of despairing prayers about global leaders and politicians, I've been praying a blessing on them. May God bless and help them be, speak, govern and act as He intended. And when someone needs physical healing, I no longer say, 'I'm not very good at that, ask someone else!' I know I have God's authority to bless them. It's not my place to tell Him exactly how, but I can listen to Him as I pray. Understanding my authority to bless keeps my eyes on Him rather than on my inadequacy. He's doing it, not me!

....

For prayer
and reflection

....

**Pray for someone
now, inviting God's
blessing on them.
Can you speak that
over them later, or
put it in writing for
them?**

Always **for us** in God's presence

Hebrews 9:22–28

'Christ... entered heaven itself, now to appear for us in God's presence.' (v24)

Whether you are giving or receiving a blessing, have you ever considered that it's the opposite of a curse, and much more powerful? Blessings don't judge, writing someone off as a fool, as disgusting or evil. Instead, they open us up to God's best.

We bless in Jesus' name. Jesus, who lives constantly in God's presence, is there for us in the throne room of His Father, Almighty God, praying for us now! Romans 8:34 says, 'Christ Jesus who died – more than that, who was raised to life – is at the right hand of God and is also interceding for us.' Paul goes on to say that nothing can separate us from God's love.

It's hard to imagine the closeness of Jesus to His Father in this life – we'll understand and experience more in the next. Meanwhile, remember that Jesus, shortly before He died, prayed for His close disciples and for those 'who will believe in me through their message': 'Holy Father, protect them by the power of your name, the name you gave me, so that they may be one as we are one' (John 17:11). Psalm 133:1,3 says: 'How good and pleasant it is when God's people live together in unity... there the LORD bestows his blessing, even life for evermore.' Jesus is still praying that for you and for me today. God wants us together, as close to Him as the persons of the Trinity are to each other, enjoying one another's presence and working together in perfect harmony. Jesus earnt the right to replace curses with His blessings, replacing curses of discord, division and pain with the harmony, unity and *shalom* peace, the wholeness and integrity of God.

For prayer and reflection

Just think: Jesus' prayers from God's throne room help empower us to live, grow and move and be one in Him!

**2 Corinthians
2:1–17**

'God… uses us to
spread the aroma
of the knowledge
of him everywhere.'
(v14)

Spreading signs of God's presence

A bottle of lavender oil broke in a shop where my daughter was working; for years afterwards, she'd keep sneezing violently at the merest whiff of its scent! Smells travel in the wind and affect deep, unconscious parts of our brains, repelling or attracting. *The Message* version translates verse 14 like this: 'Through us, he brings knowledge of Christ. Everywhere we go, people breathe in the exquisite fragrance.' Those living humbly in God's presence will attract some people; or, as Paul puts it, the presence of Christ in us will allure those who are already 'on the way of salvation' as precious perfume would. A miserably pious, judgmental hypocrite 'stinks', repelling almost everyone! So, is your aroma good or bad? Remember that Paul, and Jesus, antagonised as well as attracted many. Those who are truly carrying the presence of Jesus will smell good to God, and very bad to anyone who despises His Son.

Who drew you to Christ, and how? Maybe they didn't even *speak* about Him. Sometimes all we need to do is to be there and make space for Him. Sometimes we do have to use words – a great responsibility – but God, who enables us to carry His presence, has also equipped us and will give us the words to say: 'We stand in Christ's presence when we speak; God looks us in the face. We get what we say straight from God and say it as honestly as we can' (v17).

All of this sounds great, but can also feel like quite a responsibility. It's worth asking ourselves, who are we attracting to Jesus? Is there someone in particular He is placing on your heart? Remember, we do nothing without His help!

**For prayer
and reflection**

Lord, help all of
us all make Your
goodness more
evident in our lives,
speak out for You
boldly and
channel Your love
to others. Amen.

God's presence through **us**

1 Peter 2:1–10

find it encouraging that we're not called to our task alone. Peter uses the picture-language of Christians being brought together as 'living stones' and then built into a 'temple' that is full of God's manifest presence. He goes on to say: 'You are a chosen people, a royal priesthood, a holy nation… that you may declare the praises of him who called you out of darkness into his wonderful light' (v9). Of course, groups can convey an altogether wrong image of what God is like, as various churches have done at times throughout history. Some kept God's manifest presence to themselves, welcoming only those they considered suitable – whereas Scripture makes it clear that God wants us to invite people into, not exclude them from, His presence. I love it when God's presence bursts out of church buildings and is made evident through followers from different church traditions working together – for example, as street pastors, through food banks, debt counselling services or in prisons.

God calls some to travel in ones or twos to spread His good news; others to stay, serve and love in the spot where He's placed them. Wherever He wants us, we're working through His authority, not our own. And He's given us the assurance of His presence with us, always. Jesus' last words on earth were: 'All authority in heaven and on earth has been given to me. Therefore go and make disciples of all nations, baptising them in the name of the Father and of the Son and of the Holy Spirit, and teaching them to obey everything I have commanded you' (Matt. 28:18–20).

'you also, like living stones, are being built into a spiritual house to be a holy priesthood' (v5)

For prayer and reflection

'Jesus, You promised, 'Surely I am with you always, to the very end of the age.' Thank You. Amen.

Ludivine Kadimba

Ludivine talks to Inspiring Women about how her faith has transformed her life.

....

'Wow, God! Why me?' My immediate thoughts when asked to write for IWED. This is how I'm accustomed to think about myself. Growing up, I suffered from a low self-esteem and had little self-confidence. I didn't think much of myself.

This had much to do with family background. I can still hear dad's words resonating in my head, 'Where we come from, folk aren't meant to amount to much. Education, my poor Ludivine, it's not for us!' So, we were not to see ourselves as achievers because we were working class; from generations of manual workers. I was told this repeatedly. My better-off cousins avoided us and reinforced my experience of the social divide. They ignored us for a reason; status and reputation.

Then to this add, alcohol addiction, poverty and my care givers' poor morals and a deep sense of shame impacted my whole life. I was withdrawn, socially anxious and non-assertive. Coming to the UK from France aged nineteen, without a plan and having dropped out of school, I became a single mum within four years. The fruit of an abusive relationship, I fell on my knees asking God to help me escape my bleak outlook and gloomy destiny.

I'd believed in God 'by accident'.

Presented in his presence

I soon realised that whilst I had good intentions, I also tended to be pulled down under the influence of others. I focussed my prayer on relationships. Little more than a year later, I met my husband, a Christian, and discovered a new world. Until then, I'd believed in God 'by accident'. I wasn't raised a Christian and my parents weren't Christians. I was 'born again' in 2003, just before the birth of my second child. I grew in faith emotionally and by discovering who Jesus is and what his life and death meant for me. Gradually, my gloominess lifted, and I realised I had power over my destiny.

My husband encouraged me to enrol on a college degree course. For a mother of two, leaving the house to study felt leisurely. I enjoyed it so much, I went on to complete my PGCE and entered teaching. I then studied for my MSc. in NGO and Development Management. On the family front, I had two more children and juggled my studies, part-time work and raising a family.

Today, I'm the wellbeing group coordinator at Kintsugi Hope, a charity which creates safe and supportive spaces for people struggling with mental and emotional health challenges. In partnership with over 130 churches nationally, we offer training to people of faith to run wellbeing groups in their church and community. Here everyone is encouraged to share about their struggles in a non-judgemental context. Each week's topic is relevant to what all of us may experience during our life; shame, anger, loss, disappointment, self-acceptance, anxiety and depression. It is truly liberating! This has helped me better understand myself and, whilst I recognise and accept my own vulnerability, I've been transformed by my faith and take my role in shaping my destiny seriously.

....

Presented in His presence

....

Jude 1:20–25

'To him who is able… to present you before his glorious presence without fault and with great joy.' (v24)

The first part of Jude's short letter is an invective against immorality – grumbling, fault-finding and greed. Then hope arrives in the form of the Holy Spirit, faith, prayer and God's mercy. Finally comes the glorious declaration in verse 24. Most of us fail. Yet, through His redeeming death, Jesus brings us into God's glorious presence and life eternal. Me, presented in God's presence without fault? It doesn't sound possible without considering the first part of the verse – Jesus is able! What a joyful occasion it will be, for God, for you and I and for billions of others!

Suppose you made time to enter the throne room of God in your spirit every day? Take a few moments to do that now. If you truly grasp that Jesus and the Holy Spirit are and always will be rooting for you there, might that help you to do what the Lord requires, at least, according to Micah 6:8 – 'To act justly and to love mercy and to walk humbly with your God'?

....

Optional further reading

John 10:1–30, especially vv27–29
Brother Lawrence, *The Practice of the Presence of God* (any edition)

Restoring Our Cutting Edge

ANNE LE TISSIER

We've just read a rather unusual story, which introduces our theme for the weeks ahead: a young man fails to check the condition of a loaned axe, launches a hefty chop, then watches aghast as its cutting edge flies into the river. Iron was extremely expensive and students considerably poor; his only option was to enslave himself until the cost was repaid... but for divine intervention. I love this story, not just for its astounding ending, but for what it can teach us if we sense we have lost our spiritual 'cutting edge'.

We have the 'seal' of the indwelling Holy Spirit that cannot be taken from us, guaranteeing our heavenly inheritance. A 'cutting edge', however, is a sharp, effective or advantageous quality. Spiritually, it may be likened to the manifestation of God's power through our lives, the revelation of His character and our devotion to His purpose. So, unlike the seal of our salvation it *can* be blunted or lost, but with divine intervention, can also be restored. That's why the apostle Paul urges us to live out our lives in Christ; to grow and mature spiritually through a reverent, devoted and proactive response to all God is, all He has done, and all He still wants to do through us (Phil. 2:12–13).

I know how it feels to be like the man in the story who has lost his cutting edge and is crying out in despair. I've also known God's gracious redemption and am still learning how to keep that cutting edge sharp. I hope that together we will further explore our cutting-edge life in Jesus, how we might lose it, how God may restore it, and guidelines to help us maintain it.

2 Kings 6:1–7

'As one of them was cutting down a tree, the iron axe-head fell into the water.' (v5)

For prayer and reflection

Ungodly habits? Diluted devotion? Disinterest? Busyness? Please show me, Lord, any signs that suggest I might be losing my cutting edge, and how You wish to restore it. Amen.

A **distinguishing** feature

Exodus 33:1–17

'What else will distinguish me and your people from all the other people on the… earth?' (v16)

Have you noticed how life likes to label us, distinguishing us as one type compared to another? Extrovert or introvert; married or single; healthy or sick; young or old... Labels can be unhelpful in the way they inform our identity, set our goals, or shape our behaviour and responses. Moses, however, reminds us of our most important distinguishing feature: the presence of God in our life.

'Christ' means 'anointed one', so we are anointed by His presence indwelling our lives. But anointing also speaks of His empowering – our spiritual cutting edge. Moses knew he could not lead, nor the people succeed, without God's accompanying presence, a truth that still applies today.

The anointing of Jesus distinguishes us as His disciples. It is His presence revealing and demonstrating who He is and drawing others to Him. It transforms a kindness into the message that God sees, loves and cares for the recipient. It inspires the right word to encourage, comfort or shed light into someone's darkness. It is the divine enabling to do what we are naturally incapable of.

For prayer and reflection

Forgive me, Lord, when I live within the boundaries of my capability. Help me raise my awareness of, and dependency on, the anointing of Your presence at all times. Amen.

In our 'cover story' this month, Elisha's student-disciples had been affirmed with the blessing of the man of God (2 Kings 6:2), but that wasn't enough for them. They also asked, 'Won't you please come with your servants?' (6:3). Just because we believe in the anointing of Christ, we too may still need to nurture an intentional focus on His presence, which, in turn, raises our felt dependency on Him to empower the things we do. After all, without Him we can do nothing of significance for His kingdom (John 15:5).

It **wouldn't happen** to me

'So, if you think
you are standing
firm, be careful
that you don't fall!'
(10:12)

My life has seen changing seasons from intimate devotion to Jesus and vibrant growing faith, to disillusionment and spiritual barrenness or neglect. Perhaps you too have known times when you've been passionate for God's holiness, bold in your witness and taken steps of faith beyond your natural capability. But you've also known periods when you dragged your feet through the motions of serving the Lord, when enthusiasm for prayer dulled; or when the comforts of the world proved more alluring and its goals esteemed more worthwhile than pursuing the kingdom of God. Seasons when your head belief was just that – a belief that was barely impacting the detail of everyday life.

Some of us may be in such a season today, our life bearing signs suggesting that we've lost our cutting edge of life in Christ. The rest of us, however, may simply need the gentle reminder that no matter how passionate for Jesus we are, no one is immune to letting that slip. The demands or problems of daily life, our spiritual enemy, or our self-driven nature can all play their part in undermining the transforming, empowering, influential potential of yielding to the presence of God.

The good news is that if we're aware of a spiritual bluntness or dullness, God longs to restore the fullness of His life to us. And even if we feel spiritually sharp, I hope these notes will help us encourage floundering friends, or highlight any warning signs to take heed of ourselves. So, let's seek to run our race of life with perseverance and purpose, as we consider how to take care of the unsurpassed, priceless anointing of God.

**For prayer
and reflection**

**Be honest with
God about how
you're feeling
regarding your life
in Him. Then pray:
Lord, please help
me restore Your
perspective, peace
and power through
Jesus. Amen.**

The cutting edge of **conviction**

Luke 22:31–34, 54–62

'The Lord turned and looked straight at Peter… And he went outside and wept bitterly' (vv61–62)

P eter was convinced he would never fail Jesus. Blinded by self-assurance, he couldn't see what was happening as once, twice, then three times he denied knowing or being with Him. But then the cock crowed, and their eyes met across the crowd.

See, hear and feel Peter's wretched conviction.

Denying Jesus appears in many guises; perhaps through disobedience, self-focused pursuits, or simply choosing to ignore Him. Whether we deny Him once, twice or a hundred times, a moment will come when we sense Him staring into the depth of our soul, and realisation dawns.

'Oh no, my lord!' the student cried out when he lost his cutting edge (2 Kings 6:5); a few short words, which can sound like little more than a comedic cuss, but this was no 'oops,' or 'whoops-a-daisy'. He was highly agitated with a stomach-wrenching, heart-pounding distress. A sincere regret for not taking better care of the tool. But, thankfully, he looked to the right place for help.

As well as a cutting edge to life in Christ, there is a cutting edge to the Holy Spirit's conviction, unlike the blunted shaming and blaming condemnation of our enemy. So, just as the students asked Elisha to accompany them, and Peter followed Jesus to the Sanhedrin, be encouraged that in seeking to remain close to God we will more promptly discern His conviction. And when God makes us aware of something that disowns or contradicts Him, let's receive it for the gift that it is. God does not convict to disgrace or disempower. He disciplines us to help us restore our spiritual cutting edge – the empowered, influential life we can live in Jesus.

For prayer and reflection

Thank You, Lord, for Your precise, immediate conviction, and my assured hope of forgiveness as I make myself right with You. Amen.

A word for the disinterested

I do hope that God is already speaking to you in some way through these notes. Perhaps for some of us, however, this study has yet to ignite a response, especially if we have no felt longing for a greater encounter of the promises on offer from our life in Christ. Our lives may be so good, or so problematic, that Christ's promise of spiritual 'life to the full' to impact our daily routine has yet to inspire us. But God, in His infinite love, will never stop reaching out with immeasurably more of Himself than we can imagine, to equip our natural physical life with the empowering of His presence. So, let's consider Jesus' question: 'Who do you say I am?'

When we can answer with our heart and not just our head, 'You are the Messiah, the Son of the living God', we affirm within our whole being that Jesus is our true source of life, inviting Him to permeate the truth deep within that He gives value, purpose, hope and empowering to our life in the world. And that kind of awareness cannot help but inflame a longing for more.

If, however, you still lack a felt passion for Jesus, then let me share this: when I find myself distracted from or disinterested in the spiritual blessings of my life in Christ, I pause to imagine myself outside the empty tomb, and how I would feel if I was looking at the crucified Jesus, standing before me. Alive. There are times when the impact is so powerful that I fall to my knees in tearful, loving gratitude. But the one thing this exercise always does, is arouse my desire for more of His life. Perhaps this might help you too.

For prayer and reflection

'Consider him... so that you will not grow weary and lose heart' (Heb. 12:3). Take time now to ponder who Jesus is, and how that inspires your response.

What do I fear losing most?

....

Luke 2:41–52

'Thinking he was in their company, they travelled on for a day.'
(v44)

The family faced a 60+ mile journey back to Nazareth. If the rain held off and the tracks remained dry, they might just be home in five days. At first, the journey was slow, but as the multitude of pilgrims began to disperse off the main road heading north to their own towns and villages, Joseph and Mary were able to up their pace. But where was Jesus?

Perhaps we can resonate with the nauseating, gut-wrenching panic as they 'anxiously' searched for Him. But I wonder if this is a fear we would feel if, through our assumptions, distractions, routine or goals, we lost the special anointing presence of God, and whether that would be important to us.

Take time this weekend to sit somewhere quiet and comfortable and reflect on these questions: Is the presence of Jesus (the theme of last month's notes) a central part of my focus and dependency, a safety net in the background 'for emergencies', or have I lost sight of Him completely? Who or what else am I putting my trust and security in for life's journey?

Be assured, Jesus is waiting for you to re-join Him on His Father's business. He is for you, not against you.

....

Optional further reading
R.T. Kendall, *The Sensitivity of the Spirit* (Lake Mary, FL, USA: Charisma House, 2001)

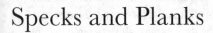

Specks and Planks

NEW book from Jeff Lucas

'Excuse me, I think there is a speck of
sawdust in your eye. I'll help you remove
it… just need to move this plank to one
side.' This collection of stories by Jeff will
amuse, challenge and – when tempted
to display speck-hunting and plank-
protruding behaviour – motivate all of us
to show more kindness and be less swift to
judge. With some stories written during the
early months of the coronavirus pandemic,
we will also remember that, in times of
uncertainty and worry, hope and help are
only a prayer away.

Find out more at
**waverleyabbeyresources.org/
specksandplanks**

2 Kings 6:1–7

'"Where did it fall?"… Elisha cut a stick and threw it there, and made the iron float.' (v6)

'Oh no, **my lord**!'

magine if our story concluded with the despairing student disappearing over the horizon, enslaved by the consequence of his mistake. It would be a sorry picture indeed, but it does not have to be ours if we ask and receive God's help to restore our spiritual cutting edge.

Wood floats; iron sinks. It was impossible, naturally speaking, for the stick Elisha threw on the water to nose-dive into the dark depths, slot itself into the hole of the axe-head, and then resurface. But the stick, like the wooden cross of Jesus, symbolises God's power required to restore what had been lost. We are no more able to pay the price to restore our spiritual cutting edge in Christ than the poor student could afford new iron. Jesus alone can do that for us.

Jesus didn't just die for the sins we committed before we declared Him the Son of God. He died for all our failures – past, present and future. The stick emerged with the iron from the river, but Jesus rose miraculously from the darkness of a tomb, offering us the miracle of restoration we need today. So, when we become enslaved by a sin or despair over some kind of failure, or find ourselves fumbling and groping without success to restore what we've lost, let's be encouraged to cry out for God's help, and take hold of it. Let's choose to reach out for the promises, presence, provision and counsel God wants to restore to us. Our transforming, empowering life in Christ is not something to receive passively, but with intentional focus and response. And let's prepare our hearts in prayer for an open and willing response to God's prompts over the coming days.

For prayer and reflection

'Create in me a pure heart, O God, and renew a steadfast spirit within me… Restore to me the joy of your salvation' (Psa. 51:10,12). Amen.

Lost through wrong **priorities**

Luke 10:38–42

'Mary has chosen what is better, and it will not be taken away from her.'
(v42)

Whatever 'preparations' Martha was entrenched in serving Jesus, they made her flustered and stressed, but she dumped her frustration and blame on Mary. I can certainly relate to her angst as I juggle time and energy for the many responsibilities that I feel I have. But Jesus gently diffused her rant with the truth. Mary had chosen the best thing to prioritise – simply being with Jesus and listening to Him; the only thing that would transform and empower her to live effectively for Him.

Our cover story reads, 'As one of them was cutting down a tree, the iron axe-head fell into the water' (2 Kings 6:5). It all sounds very sudden, the loss of the student's cutting edge, but the warning signs would have been there for some time. Axes used for cutting trees had a wooden handle, slotted through a hole in the iron head then fastened together with leather straps. It was a common problem for the straps to deteriorate or loosen and the iron to fly off, which suggests it was also common practice to check the straps first (see Deut. 19:5). If Elisha's young student had been as concerned about the tool – the fundamental equipping for his job – as he was concerned about the job itself, he may have noticed the weaknesses appearing in the straps, and taken time to mend them.

What about you – how are the 'straps' that keep your spiritual cutting edge in place? Do you need to take time out with Jesus to maintain His enabling for the tasks He has called you to do? Unlike Mary, we don't leave Jesus behind in another room but are called to serve with Him, through the presence of His Spirit.

For prayer and reflection

Here I am Lord, sitting at Your feet. Gazing. Listening. Open and receptive to Your presence. Guide, counsel and enrich me as You wish. Amen.

Lost through **discouragement**

1 Kings 19:1–18

'I have had enough, LORD' (v4)

When my brother battled with alcoholism, I questioned why God didn't seem to answer my prayers for healing. When I was left feeling bruised and shamed from being slandered by someone close to me, I struggled to understand why God did not intervene. I felt Elijah's despair, saying, 'Lord, I've had enough.'

David wrote, 'My heart is in anguish within me; the terrors of death have fallen on me. Fear and trembling have beset me; horror has overwhelmed me' (Psa. 55:4–5). If this describes how we're feeling today, we have a choice. We can doubt and give up on our Father God, despite the fact that in Him are the answers we look for: wisdom, fortitude, comfort, justification, and at times, divine intervention. Or else, we can 'Cast [our] cares on the LORD' – holding them out before Him in prayer, believing in who we know God to be, trusting with every fibre of our being in His promises, 'and he will sustain [us]; he will never let the righteous be shaken' (Psa. 55:22).

We all suffer from the effects of an imperfect world and from behaviour which hurts or harms us. If you resonate with Elijah's response to his problems that caused him to run away from trusting God, notice how God never let him out of His sight. He offered Elijah nourishment and Elijah chose to receive it. He offered His sustaining presence and Elijah chose to be present to it. He gave guidance that offered support for the present and the future, and Elijah acted upon it.

God is offering you spiritual nourishment, His reassuring presence, His guidance to sustain you. Receive His hand reaching out to you – and reach out your heart to Him.

For prayer and reflection

Let nothing rob you of your cutting edge life in Christ. Mull on scripture; let it feed your soul. Still your thoughts to focus on God. Respond to what He shows you.

Lost through **negativity**

**Ephesians
4:17–32**

'be made new in
the attitude of your
minds' (v23)

I n a matter of minutes, the woman sitting next to me had sapped every drop of my energy. She had complained she couldn't hear last night's talk from her backrow seat, grumbled about the food being served, moaned about her poor night's sleep and criticised her church for a whole host of reasons.

We can all be tempted to moan and complain at times, instead of reflecting the attitudes of the early disciples of Christ whose behaviour and speech were being moulded by His. It was a moment of deep personal challenge for me: what negative and critical attitudes had *I* allowed to fester, which dulled the cutting edge life of the Holy Spirit in me?

Negative attitudes show up in many guises, so here are a few examples. Believing we are never good enough, feeling inferior to others or putting ourselves down. Replaying all the times we've messed up. Jumping to negative conclusions without knowing the facts. Allowing a critical, judgmental, grumbling, complaining, self-righteous outlook.

While many of us may occasionally struggle with thoughts or attitudes like this, remember that they can undermine the essence of the God we say we believe in, and mask the truth of His presence in our life. Let's choose instead to build others up, to be an encourager, to speak positively without ending the sentence with 'but...' Choose to see life and people through the lens of God's love, grace, faithfulness, provision, forgiveness, humility, care and support, and so fill up a room with vibrant joy, love and faith.

**For prayer
and reflection**

For many years this quote has helped reshape my outlook: 'There is no such thing as bad weather, just inappropriate clothing.' What attitude are you stirred to embrace?

Lost through **worldliness**

Titus 2:11–3:8

'For the grace of God… teaches us to… live self-controlled, upright and godly lives in this present age' (2:11–12)

I n my book *Restoring the Balance*,* I explain how I became a Christian in my mid-teens but let my devotion lapse after a few years. I never lost my faith, but my beliefs had no impact on the way I lived: drinking, inappropriate behaviour and relationships, and prioritising career goals that were far removed from God's purpose for me. During this period, I lost the cutting edge of my life in Christ; my revelation of and influence for Him, rusting in the murky depths of the worldly habits I had conformed to.

God's grace offers His undeserved gift of salvation and the power to live a life that reflects who He is. It teaches us – it instructs, encourages and corrects us – as we yield to His presence. Godliness is not driven by a need to appease a demanding God, nor to earn the favour of a loving heavenly Father, but demonstrates who our first love is; who or what we most long to please, delight and honour. Saying 'no' to the habits, choices, words and behaviour that deny God's character and will is saying 'yes' to loving Jesus, 'yes' to the love God has lavished on us, 'yes' to living out the nature of kingdom life. It says 'yes' to a desire to live life with the cutting edge of His Spirit-empowered influence, as He transforms us increasingly into His likeness and equips us with everything we need to do His will.

In what ways might the Holy Spirit be prompting your response to the presence and implications of God's grace – in regard to your own conduct, to how you treat and relate to others, and in your devotion to God Himself?

**Restoring the Balance* (Farnham: CWR, 2019)

For prayer and reflection

How easily I call You my first love, Lord, yet deny it in practice. I do love You. Please show me what dulls the revelation and power of Your life in me. Amen.

Weekend

What are my weaknesses?

....

2 Samuel 11:1–17

'David got up from his bed and walked around on the roof of the palace… he saw a woman washing.' (v2)

srael's annual harvest should have been a good cause for celebration, but the farmers' gratitude was tinged with fear as enemies appeared at the borders, threatening to steal their grain. It was necessary for David to fulfil his role in leading the troops to defend God's people. But David remained in the comfort of his palace, entertaining himself elsewhere…

We might never imagine succumbing to murder, but Paul cautions that we can all give in to some kind of temptation, with potential to lose the cutting edge of our life in Christ (1 Cor. 10:11–13). So, let's consider the following: David neglected the role God had chosen him for – *what excuse am I tempted to make to avoid being where God wants me to be?* David entertained his temptation – *what are my weaknesses? How can I avoid or nip temptation early?* David tried to cover up the consequences – *what private habits am I hiding, or what do I say to mask the real version of the truth?*

Consider how your answers may help strengthen your holy response and relationship with your loving Father.

....

Optional further reading

Matthew 4:1–11; 1 Corinthians 9:24–25; 10:11–13

Get your FRE

From January 2021 your favourite Bible Reading notes will be available to you for FREE. God has called us back to the original vision of CWR to provide these notes to everyone who needs them, regardless of their circumstance or ability to pay.

It is our desire to see these daily bible reading notes used more widely, to see Christians grow in their relationship with Jesus on a daily basis and to see Him reflected in their everyday living.

Mary recently wrote saying 'I just want to say how much I have appreciated *Every Day with Jesus*. My husband has some very serious medical problems and, on top of this, has dementia. Since the lockdown, his dementia has worsened considerably and we have been unable to go out, obviously no-one is allowed to visit us, so the full responsibility of care falls to me. Thankfully, with *Every Day with Jesus*, I have been able to grab a few moments of blessing and peace each day, knowing that our Lord is fully within my situation and is walking the walk with me'.

More than 60,000 copies each year are delivered into prisons too and our vision is to grow this ministry even further, putting these notes into the hands of those in challenging situations and to see their lives transformed through a new and growing relationship with Jesus.

David, an ex-prisoner said 'Thank you so much for your generous gift of *Every Day with Jesus*. Whilst in prison each issue spoke to me where I was emotionally and mentally at the time. Each copy helped me to feel loved, despite all my sin and rejection. It's not that I've never been loved, I've just never allowed myself to feel it. Now love has filled me up and overflows out of me. I thank God for your work, because, by your work, gifted from God, you've helped another sinner for which I'll be eternally grateful'.

Clearly there are costs to provide this ministry and we are trusting in God's provision. Could you be part of this vision? Do you have the desire to see lives transformed through a relationship with Jesus? **A small donation from you of just £2 a month, by direct debit, will make such a difference.** Giving hope to someone in desperate need whilst you too grow deeper in your own relationship with Jesus.

Lost through **hindrances**

**Ephesians
1:3,18–20;
Hebrews 12:1–3**

'let us throw off
everything that
hinders'
(Heb. 12:1)

Spiritual blessings and heavenly riches may sound a tad surreal compared to the pressures of paying the bills, health issues, infertility, grief and pain. Our daily routines, responsibilities and relationships can feel so demanding or mundane, overwhelming or trivial, rewarding or worthless, that they distract us from the greater reality of our supernatural lives in Christ. And yet, Jesus offers us the mind-blowing truth of spiritual life 'to the full' – in abundance, to overflowing (John 10:10); spiritual blessings which are God's gifts to sustain and equip us, to influence, empower and overflow our natural lives – in turn, revealing His presence to others.

To 'throw off', therefore, is to be intentional about letting go of whatever may have blunted our experience of this spiritual cutting edge we have in Christ. Hebrews describes sin as something that 'entangles' (constrains and interferes with the freedom and full impact of the life of God's Spirit within). We looked at this on Friday, but the things that 'hinder' come in many guises: fear of losing out on the pleasures of this world if we pursue God's priorities; doubts about God's faithfulness; scepticism about spiritual realities; unwillingness to be God's instrument; or the 'stuff' of life (TV, social media, overloaded schedules, misplaced priorities) that steal our time, attention, energy, focus, gifting and resources away from life in Jesus, in favour of less meaningful pursuits. Consider what you may need to resist or discard to encounter a greater measure of 'life to the full'.

**For prayer
and reflection**

Lord, I want to
grasp hold of my
life in You in greater
measure. Help me
identify whatever I
need to throw off
that may be
undermining my
relationship with
You. Amen.

Lost through **misplaced goals**

I have stopped making long-term goals because I found they gave me a false sense of being in control of my life, not God – and would often end up defining how I measured success, not necessarily reflecting His objectives.

God's Word conveys every goal we can aspire to fulfil in character and purpose. There is still a place for diligence; planning how we might fulfil God's goal to share with the needy, for example, how to offer hospitality, or organise working schedules to make the most of our God-given potential. But as we pursue *His* goals, we can trust Him to fulfil all that He wants to do through our lives, including the roles He has specifically called us to.

We have some immense promises regarding our life in Christ, and some awesome goals to realise as a result of our union with Him (see John 15:5–16). But these promises depend on us yielding to His ways and His words. The definition of godly success, therefore, equates to the depth of our devotion to Jesus and our dedication to living a life that pleases Him, rather than specific 'results'. His success for us will arise through the extent to which our lives are aligned and proactively responding to His character and commands, His priorities and purpose.

Consider whether your own goals are pursuing God's character and purpose, are shaped and directed by Scripture, or clearly confirmed by a prophetic word. And if you are unsure, then be encouraged that as you choose to prioritise knowing Jesus, to love and be loved by Him and to be open to a greater encounter of His presence, God's goals for you will surface.

2 Corinthians 5:1–10; Philippians 3:7–14

'So we make it our goal to please him' (2 Cor. 5:9)

For prayer and reflection

Forgive me, Lord, when I've prayed 'Your kingdom come' but pursued 'my kingdom come'. The one thing I now seek as my priority, is You. Amen.

Lost through **indifference**

2 Kings 13:14–19

'You should have
struck the ground
five or six times'
(v19)

E lisha clearly explained the symbolism of victory through the shooting of the first arrow. And yet, when Jehoash was invited to claim as many victories as he had arrows – the number of battles needed by Israel's small army to completely destroy the vast Aramean ranks – he stopped short. By striking the ground with just three arrows from his quiver, he showed a limited enthusiasm that would prove insufficient for the task; that was inadequate to realise the fullness of God's promised victory (v19).

Some of us may have lost our cutting edge anointing for similar reasons. We might want complete victory but are unwilling to give the time, effort, faith or devotion required to see God's promises accomplished in full measure. In fact, this story once had a profound effect on me. I had been given a waistcoat as a prophetic symbol of God's anointing to teach His Word. Being extremely introverted, however, and preferring homemaking and the pastoral setting to speaking from a platform, I had hidden it in a drawer; I had effectively buried the potential of the anointing by not pursuing God's promise in full measure.

A reluctancy to put in the time and work needed to pursue God's call, a disinterest in His priorities, or giving into fear – the feeling we cannot trust God – are just a few ways we can dilute our enthusiasm for Him. These are potential underlying causes why we may not be experiencing some of the promises in His Word or the full measure of a prophetic word spoken over us. If you sense your passion for God and His purposes has cooled, prayerfully consider the reasons why that may be.

**For prayer
and reflection**

Lord, please forgive
me for diluting my
potential with by
doubts, distractions
and worldly
priorities, instead
of passionately
pursuing my life
in You. Amen.

Where did it fall?

After years of living in rented accommodation and then a church-owned house, I was elated when God clearly led us to buy our own home. The problem was, I soon fell in love with the gift more than the Giver, which in turn, dulled the anointing of His Spirit through my life, though it took me some time to notice!

'Where did it fall?' Elisha asked (2 Kings 6:6). I've suggested some potential answers in these notes, but it's not always easy to pinpoint what dulled our first love for Jesus, doused the flames of our passion to pursue His priorities, or lowered our desire to share His truth with those who don't know Him. It may have been a one-off event; the sudden passing of a loved one or a falling out with a church leader, for example. We may have lost it over time, so distracted or enamoured by other pursuits that we stopped taking time to sharpen the blade – to nurture our relationship with Jesus. Or maybe we never noticed it had disappeared at all, hacking unsuccessfully at our 'tree' in a blind attempt to achieve the impossible in our own strength and ability.

If you still need help to discern how you lost God's anointing, just ask Him. He knows us far better than we know ourselves. He sees the motives of our hearts and understands the 'why' behind the things that lure us away. So be encouraged to ask with a receptive heart and mind, believing that God will answer. He deeply loves and longs for you to be restored to abundant life in Him.

From tomorrow, we will move on with our story, reflecting on important principles to restore, encourage and maintain our awesome encounter of life in Christ.

Psalm 139:1–18,23–24

'You have searched me, LORD, and you know me… you perceive my thoughts from afar.' (vv1–2)

For prayer and reflection

'Search me, God, and know my heart… See if there is any offensive way in me, and lead me in the way everlasting' (Psa. 139:23–24). Amen.

My Father, **my restorer**

Luke 15:11–31

'When he came to his senses, he said… "I will set out and go back to my father"' (vv17–18)

mentioned on Wednesday that God's purpose for me to teach His Word had been clearly conveyed: first through a prophetic word and symbol, long before I prepped any sermons or conference talks, and then, roughly seven years later, through Scripture. After accepting the calling and growing in it for some years, however, I then abandoned it, choosing to live by my fears rather than faith.

The moment I sensed God's conviction, a new fear gripped my heart: would He ever be able to trust me again with this work? Through countless tears I held on to my belief in God's forgiveness. Over many months, I learned to forgive myself. But whether God would restore this specific anointing remained unknown.

God does not delay in forgiving our heart's confession, and for some, like Elisha's servant, He restores His cutting edge enabling for a task immediately: 'When he showed him the place, Elisha cut a stick and threw it there, and made the iron float. "Lift it out," he said. Then the man reached out his hand and took it' (2 Kings 6:6–7). For others, God may restore a different anointing, perhaps equipping them for a new role. And for those like me, there may be a waiting period. This is not a time to get stuck in regret, but a time to grieve the loss, turn from the choices or attitudes that brought it about, learn and in turn grow from the mistakes.

If you now find yourself at this point of conviction and grief, be reassured. As today's reading reminds us, God watches and waits for us to return to Him, to help us re-engage with the inheritance we already have in Christ, as God's cherished child.

For prayer and reflection

Merciful Father, I have wrestled with my thoughts and fears about my mistakes for too long. I trust You to restore Your anointing, in Your chosen time and way. Amen.

MAR/APR 2021

March

THE PLACE OF REST

CAROL HERZIG

April

SHAMELESS

REBECCA BERRY

In **March**, Carol Herzig helps us to find our place of rest in the Lord, enabling us to respond with godly perspectives, and to grow in the Lord's peace, joy and thankfulness.

In **April**, Rebecca Berry explores the shamelessness of Jesus, and how His death and resurrection has enabled us to be redeemed, forgiven, joyful and shameless people.

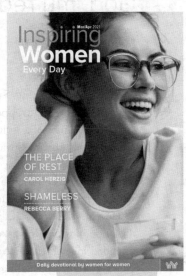

Inspiring
Women
Every Day

THE PLACE
OF REST
CAROL HERZIG

SHAMELESS
REBECCA BERRY

Daily devotional by women for women

Also available as eBook/eSubscription

Obtain your copy from Waverley Abbey Resources, Christian bookshops or your National Distributor.
If you would like to take out a subscription, see the order form at the back of these notes.

Weekend

God, my redeemer

....

Jonah 1:1–17; 2:1–2,10

'In my distress I called to the LORD, and he answered me.' (2:2)

Dark. Churning. Stinking. Terrifying. I know what it's like to feel trapped in what seems like the hopeless confines of a living grave, saved by God's grace but knowing that the mess was of my own making. Whether you have been in a similar place for days, months or even years, find a 'safe place' to consider the following, and grasp hold of God's strong but loving hand extended to you.

Do you find yourself, like Jonah, running in the opposite direction of what God asked you to do, or in a place He never intended for you to be? Admit where you ignored or rejected God's guidance or calling, whether that was through fear, to pursue your own plans, or for some other reason. Know, with every fibre of your being, God's forgiveness extended to you.

The redeemer of mistakes may renew your previous calling (see Jonah 3:1–3), or work through you to fulfil His will in a new way. But be assured as you wait: you are loved, valued and still have a unique role to fulfil in His kingdom purposes.

....

Optional further reading

Psalm 32; Job 19:23–27

Forgive yourself

'neither do I
condemn you…
Go now and leave
your life of sin.'
(v11)

The woman's act of adultery was no private affair. She made headline news, with a public trial to shame and indict her on the grounds of Mosaic Law. But Jesus overruled the letter of the law with God's spirit of forgiveness and redemption, saving her from the punishment of death by stoning. That said, she would still have had the 'mess' at home to return to. Her angry husband may have divorced her, leaving her without protection or provision. Her reputation would have most likely been marred for the rest of her life, unless she'd had personal funds and the means of safe travel to escape the close-knit community and begin again elsewhere.

Perhaps we have also received Christ's mercy but are struggling to forgive ourselves because we are still reaping the effects of what we have sown. I can remember when this happened to me, my life felt harassed, crushed and hampered by regret, shame, remorse, grief and implacable disappointment with myself. Not forgiving ourselves is like rejecting Christ's hand of help reaching out to us. It holds us back from experiencing the fullness of the promises of our cutting edge life in Him; the blessings of peace, comfort, hope, purpose, growth, guidance, contentment and self-worth.

The axe floated because God still had a purpose for it – and God still has a purpose for you. Christ set you free from sin and condemnation, so please don't remain chained to the life of a captive when you can choose to be kind and forgive yourself. And be encouraged, because God wants to walk through any fallout with you, which we will consider tomorrow.

For prayer and reflection

Picture the hands of Jesus unlocking you from the chains of unforgiveness. Receive His freedom to your heart, mind and emotions – and let whatever has shackled you fall.

Faith in the fallout

Jeremiah 29:1–14

'For I know the plans I have for you… plans to give you hope and a future.' (v11)

In our cover story, the consequence of the student's neglect was potential enslavement. The effects of our own errors may be a broken relationship, job loss, a marred reputation, physical damage of some kind or something else you can identify, still gnawing at your conscience in an attempt to hold you back from the cutting edge life you've been given in Christ. The Israelites in today's reading had also failed God, and had consequently been taken captive to enemy nations. But some key points arise from the broader narrative.

God commanded the exiles to pray for the people and place of their exile. Even if we have repented of our wrongdoing, we may find ourselves in a place God never planned for us to be, but He still wants to sustain and enrich us with His presence so that we, in turn, may convey His blessing to others. His love and greater purposes – which include your life – have not diminished. Furthermore, even though it was the Israelites' own sin that reaped the devastation of their lives, God took it upon Himself to restore what their sin had undone (Joel 2:25). God also encouraged them to look out for something new (Isa. 43:18–19). His nature is to bring beauty from ashes, joy from tears, praise from despair, even life from death.

God may therefore choose to mend or restore to you what was lost through sin, but He may also choose to do something new. For now, be assured that He has not abandoned you to sin's consequences. His offer of spiritual wisdom, guidance, comfort, peace and provision remains – all you need is the faith to ask and to trust Him for His good response.

For prayer and reflection

Lord, help me where I have let the fallout of past errors hold me back from trusting You with my future. Thank You for Your promises made true in Christ. Amen.

Maintaining our cutting edge

WEDS **FEB 24**

2 Peter 1:1–11

'these qualities… will keep you from being ineffective and unproductive in your knowledge of our Lord Jesus Christ.' (v8)

A story of two woodcutters is retold in a number of ways, but always concluding with the same punchline. One man chops away with his axe all day, the other takes regular breaks to rest and sharpen his blade. Much to the surprise of the first woodcutter, it is the second man, who stops working in order to take care of his cutting edge, who chops the most wood in the allocated time.

In our cover story, Elisha's student neglected to take care of the straps that fixed the wooden handle into the axe-head. Sometimes our lives can get so busy or problematic that we forget to take care of our most precious thing too – our relationship with God and our response to His presence. And though we may not watch in horror as an axe-head flies off, our relationship with God may begin to feel dull, lifeless, or sheer hard work, often with little fruit to show for it in our own lives, or in the influence we have on others.

So, let's be aware of any weak spots or vulnerable areas God has highlighted to us this month; to any steps we've felt prompted to take or any misplaced priorities we need to address. But also note, there are two key habits we have yet to consider to ensure our cutting edge life in Christ does not become 'ineffective and unproductive'.

Abraham Lincoln famously said, 'Give me six hours to chop down a tree and I will spend the first four sharpening the axe.' If we want to be honed and ready for God to use as He chooses, then we need to prioritise our relationship with Him through prayer and our response to His Word; two things we'll be considering over the next couple of days.

For prayer and reflection

Jot down any areas of your life you need to address, or action steps to take, that the Holy Spirit has prompted you with this month. Prayerfully review your response.

Our **priority** in **prayer**

Psalm 27:1–14

'One thing I ask from the LORD, this only do I seek' (v4)

W hen a bishop, so overwhelmed by his work, admitted he had little time to pray, Mother Teresa replied: 'If you are too busy to pray, you are too busy!'

Excessive hours at work, family responsibilities, hobbies, social media feeds, paying bills, food shopping, cooking, cleaning, reaching out to a friend, and a diary full of church events to lead or support, can fill up a day from 5am to midnight if we don't take control and claim back time for restoring our cutting edge life in Christ – time to engage with its source.

When David wrote this psalm, to be close to God's presence meant travelling to the Tabernacle – the ornate tent where God's Spirit dwelt among His people within the innermost sanctuary. But although we now have the presence of God's Spirit with us 24/7, this psalm constantly challenges me. The 'one thing', the deepest longing David prayed for more than anything else, was to *dwell* in the presence of the Lord.

We may think we are too busy to pray, but that depends on our priorities. If our desire or motivation to pray is to be present to God's presence, we will find a way to make it happen. Wherever we are, we can be present to God with us in that space, 'gazing... seeking', sharing the moment with Him and He with us, no matter how tired or frustrated we may initially feel.

Of course, there is a place for 'asking' in prayer for our personal needs or guidance, as well as praying for others. But prayer as a means to restore greater awareness of Jesus with us is one of the key gifts we've been given to encounter the source of our cutting edge life in Christ.

For prayer and reflection

Start by asking, as David did, to be more present to God's presence indwelling your life. Even the act of asking will begin to shift your focus onto God being with you.

The **whetstone** of God's Word

2 Timothy
3:10–17

'so that the servant
of God may be
thoroughly
equipped for every
good work' (v17)

M y husband uses a whetstone to sharpen
his axe before chopping up logs for our fire.
The process works through abrasion; the
whetstone's tiny rough-edged particles rubbing away
the chipped, blunt, grimy metal to sharpen its cutting
edge. God's Word is just like that, acting in us to shape,
shine and sharpen, so that we may be 'thoroughly
equipped'.

But the image suggests we nurture a proactive
responsiveness to God's Word, to restore or maintain
our cutting edge of life in Christ. For 'the word of God is
alive and active. Sharper than any double-edged sword,
it penetrates... it judges the thoughts and attitudes of
the heart' (Heb. 4:12). Our Bibles are not just words on
a page offering godly guidelines; the words are infused
with God's vibrant life to transform, guide and empower.

Merely studying Scripture with our intellectual
capacities imparts knowledge, but when we read
with an earnest openness, the Holy Spirit responds:
enlightening truth to our hearts and minds, discipling
and correcting attitudes or conduct that grieve rather
than please Him, transforming us increasingly into the
image of our holy Father, 'so that' we will be honed and
prepared for God's work. In fact, the whetstone of the
Word shapes, shines and sharpens us to relate, pray,
serve, work, teach, rebuke, counsel, and share our gifts
and resources wherever God chooses.

Do still read for knowledge but, to restore and
maintain your cutting edge life in Christ, read your Bible,
believing that this is a means for God to work in and
through your life (1 Thess. 2:13) – one verse at a time.

**For prayer
and reflection**

Pause each time
you read Scripture,
and pray with a
sincere heart:
'Open my eyes
that I may see
wonderful things
in your law'
(Psa. 119:18).
Amen.

Move on with peace

....

Luke 7:36–50

'Your faith has saved you; go in peace.' (v50)

M ary knew she had lived a godless life but believed what she had seen and heard about Jesus, the man infused with the presence of God to forgive and help restore her life to where God intended it to be.

If God has been speaking to you through these notes, please be encouraged to stop swinging away with a wooden handle when He is offering to restore your iron axe-head. Why keep slogging away when the joy of Jesus can be reignited? Why stay in a prison of shame or condemnation when God offers you the key? Why scramble around in the dark when you have the light of God's Word to guide and counsel? Why exhaust yourself with self-effort then drown in discouragement, when God wants to empower you for fruitful service? Why struggle with the noise and demands of life, when there is harmony to be found in Jesus, dovetailing spiritual blessings with your natural life? Whatever God is saying to you or doing in your life to restore your spiritual cutting edge, do what you can to take hold of it. Worship God with the whole of your life in whatever way you can – and 'go in peace'.

....

Optional further reading
2 Kings 6:1–7; Psalm 23

Order form

Get Your **FREE** Daily Bible Reading Notes **TODAY!** (UK ONLY)

From January 2021 your favourite Bible Reading notes will be available to you for FREE. God has called us back to the original vision of CWR to provide these notes to everyone who needs them, regardless of their circumstance or ability to pay. It is our desire to see these daily bible reading notes used more widely, to see Christians grow in their relationship with Jesus on a daily basis and to see Him reflected in their everyday living. More than 60,000 copies each year are delivered into prisons too and our vision is to grow this ministry even further, putting these notes into the hands of those in challenging situations and to see their lives transformed through a new and growing relationship with Jesus. Clearly there are costs to provide this ministry and we are trusting in God's provision.

Could you be part of this vision? Do you have the desire to see lives transformed through a relationship with Jesus? **A small donation from you of just £2 a month, by direct debit, will make such a difference** Giving hope to someone in desperate need whilst you too grow deeper in your own relationship with Jesus.

4 Easy Ways To Order

1. Visit our online store at **waverleyabbeyresources.org/store**
2. Send this form together with your payment to: **CWR, Waverley Abbey House, Waverley Lane, Farnham, Surrey GU9 8EP**
3. Phone in your credit card order: **01252 784700** (Mon–Fri, 9.30am – 4.30pm)
4. Visit a Christian bookshop

For a list of our National Distributors, who supply countries outside the UK, visit waverleyabbeyresources.org/distributors

Your Details (required for orders and donations)

Full Name:	CWR ID No. (if known):
Home Address:	
	Postcode:
Telephone No. (for queries):	Email:

Publications

TITLE	QTY	PRICE	TOTAL
	Total Publications		

UK P&P: up to £24.99 = **£2.99**; £25.00 and over = **FREE**	
Elsewhere P&P: up to £10 = **£4.95**; £10.01 – £50 = **£6.95**; £50.01 – £99.99 = **£10**; £100 and over = **£30**	
Total Publications and P&P (please allow 14 days for delivery) **A**	

Payment Details

☐ I enclose a cheque made payable to CWR for the amount of: **£** _____

☐ Please charge my credit/debit card.

Cardholder's Name (in BLOCK CAPITALS) _____

Card No. ☐☐☐☐ ☐☐☐☐ ☐☐☐☐ ☐☐☐☐

Expires End ☐☐ ☐☐   Security Code ☐☐☐

Continued overleaf >>

One off Special Gift to CWR ☐ Please send me an acknowledgement of my gift **B** [ ]

GRAND TOTAL (Total of A & B) [ ]

Gift Aid (your home address required, see overleaf)

giftaid it I am a UK taxpayer and want CWR to reclaim the tax on all my donations for the four years prior to this year **and on** all donations I make from the date of this Gift Aid declaration until further notice.*

Taxpayer's Full Name (in BLOCK CAPITALS) _____

Signature _____ **Date** _____

*I am a UK taxpayer and understand that if I pay less Income Tax and/or Capital Gains Tax than the amount of Gift Aid claimed on all my donations in that tax year it is my responsibility to pay any difference.

Your FREE Daily Bible Reading Notes Order

	Please Tick	FREE	£2 pcm	£5 pcm	£10 pcm	Other
Every Day with Jesus		☐	☐	☐	☐	☐ £
Large Print *Every Day with Jesus*		☐	☐	☐	☐	☐ £
Inspiring Women Every Day		☐	☐	☐	☐	☐ £

All CWR Bible reading notes are also available in single issue **ebook** and **email subscription** format. Visit **waverleyabbeyresources.org** for further info.

CWR Instruction to your Bank or Building Society to pay by Direct Debit

Please fill in the form and send to: CWR, Waverley Abbey House, Waverley Lane, Farnham, Surrey GU8 8EP

DIRECT Debit

Name and full postal address of your Bank or Building Society

To: The Manager _____ Bank/Building Society

Address _____

_____ Postcode

Name(s) of Account Holder(s)

Branch Sort Code

Bank/Building Society Account Number

Originator's Identification Number

4	2	0	4	8	7

Reference

Instruction to your Bank or Building Society

Please pay CWR Direct Debits from the account detailed in this Instruction subject to the safeguards assured by the Direct Debit Guarantee. I understand that this Instruction may remain with CWR and, if so, details will be passed electronically to my Bank/Building Society.

Signature(s)

Date

Banks and Building Societies may not accept Direct Debit Instructions for some types of account

💬 How would you like to hear from us?

We would love to keep you up to date on all aspects of the CWR ministry, including; new publications, events & courses as well as how you can support us.

If you **DO** want to hear from us on email, please tick here [ ] If you **DO NOT** want us to contact you by post, please tick here [ ]

You can update your preferences at any time by contacting our customer services team on 01252 784 700. You can view our privacy policy online at waverleyabbeyresources.org